A
Teeny-Tiny

CHRISTMAS
COUNTDOWN

Running Press
Hachette Book Group
1290 Avenue of the Americas, New York, NY 10104
www.runningpress.com
@Running_Press

First Edition: October 2018

Published by Running Press, an imprint of Perseus Books, LL
a subsidiary of Hachette Book Group, Inc. The Running Press
name and logo is a trademark of the Hachette Book Group.

The publisher is not responsible for websites (or their content
that are not owned by the publisher.

ISBN: 978-0-7624-6234-6

Welcome to
YOUR BEST CHRISTMAS EVER

*T*welve days of Christmas?! Get real! Christmas is the most wonderful time of the year, and you're going to try to squeeze it into 12 days? No way. If you want to do Christmas right, you need to follow a plan that goes well beyond a coupl'a geese and some leaping lords.

Housed within this book's tiny pages is your definitive guide to celebrating Christmas like it deserves to be celebrated—all month long! Consider this your play-by-play game plan for a positively perfect holiday. The countdown starts on the day after Thanksgiving (though feel free to start earlier if you're feeling extra festive) and provides inspiration, tips, and step-by-step instructions for completing all of your holiday tasks by the big day. Feel free to skip ahead or do things out of order: it's your holiday, for St. Nick's sake! And don't get overwhelmed. It's just like they always say: a tinsel tree is decorated one tinsel string at a time. You can do this!

Pour yourself a glass of eggnog (whiskey optional) and *fa la la...let's go!*

The Day after Thanksgiving

The leftover turkey is in its Tupperware, your family is gone, and sweatpants are all that fit you right now. Before you cozy up on your couch for a marathon of movies and snoozin', let's just cross a few things off the to-do-before-Christmas list, shall we?

DRAW NAMES. Now is the time to make the call: Are you doing a Pollyanna? Secret Santa? White elephant? Gifts for everyone (who do you think you are, Santa?)? Our advice: call your sister and explain that while you love getting crocheted socks every year, maybe it's time to waste not, want not and throw all the cousins', all the aunts and uncles', all the brothers and sisters' names into a hat and pick a name so everybody only has to get one present this year.

MAKE YOUR HOLIDAY CARDS.

Head to your local art supply store and buy a couple of rubber stamps—snow-flakes, Christmas trees, whatever you like—some ink, and some card stock.

Cut and fold the paper into small cards and throw a stamp on the front. Do it while you watch TV! It's super easy and will make you feel like a kid again.

GET OUT YOUR DECORATIONS.

This one is easy. You don't even have to actually *decorate*. But it is advised that you do the chore of getting your decorations out from wherever they've been living for the last 11 months: the basement, various junk drawers, the back of your closet. Get 'em out and inspect 'em. Make sure no family of mice found their way into the bags, and check that your ornament box is full of intact ornaments and not hundreds of shards of broken glass. That's it! Your day-after-Thanksgiving list is done. Take a breath, take a nap, make a few leftover Thanksgiving food sammies, and enjoy the last few days of November. December is right around the corner and it's about to get real.

DECORATE. Okay, no more messing around: It's time to get the lights up and the wreaths hung. Do it now to avoid the dreadful "What's the point in putting up decorations if Christmas is next week?" debacle. Put on Christmas music, make some hot toddies, and get it done—it's impossible to avoid the holiday spirit when you're surrounded by tinsel and glitter.

PICK OUT A TREE. Whether you're a "Pack a thermos of hot chocolate, put on your snow boots and go hunting for the perfect tree at a 'U·Cut·It' place" kind of tree shopper, a "Walk to the corner tree lot and pick one that's already cut and ready to throw on top of the car" kind of person, or a "My 'tree' lives in a box in my basement" kind of gal, you're going to have to make some choices about what kind of tree you want to display. Here's a quick run-down on your options:

* *Charlie Brown Tree* Charlie Brown trees are perfect for decorating. They may look a little sad when you first get them into your home, but there is so much space for adding flair—bulbs, lights, garland, ornaments, you name it! There's room for it to shine.

* *Big, Fat, Full Tree* The big, fat, full tree is already so beautiful, so green, you're really just sprucing it up. A cool thing about BFF trees

is that sometimes you don't even
have to hang things: if the tree
is full and fat enough, you can
sort of just stuff the ornament or
decoration into the branches and
it'll stick there. Try hiding things for
a fun holiday game!

* *Artificial Tree* Ah, artificial
trees. A real object of debate! Some
folks would never dream of putting
up an artificial tree. I suppose these
folks *really* like constantly having

to water a huge, dying plant in their living room, sweeping up needles every couple of days. Other folks love the convenience of the A.T. Do what feels right!

※ *Tinsel Tree* Popular in the 1960s, aluminum Christmas trees were the epitome of Christmas festivity and Mid-Century Modernism. The shiny, festive trees are gaining popularity once more and you can easily find them at thrift stores and even chains. They're the perfect alternative to the classic A.T. and really show the world you don't play by the dang rules.

* *Teeny-Tiny Tinsel Tree*

Crunched for time, space, or both? Never fear! The teeny-tiny tinsel tree housed in this box has so much heart, so much spirit, it is perfectly acceptable to use as your one and only Christmas tree this year. Plop it on your mantel, side table, desk, or any shelf; point the rotating color light at its shiny branches; and dress it with the provided red beads. Glorious! No one will miss the full-size tree, promise.

BEGIN CHRISTMAS DIET. Forget the bikini body diet, it's time to get Christmas cookie ready. How, you ask? Simple. Start upping your intake of sugar, butter, and carbs now. Usually you have a smoothie for breakfast? That's nice. Time to switch to donuts. A green salad for lunch? Fine, but no lunch is complete without one, maybe two, cookies to cleanse the palette. And your afternoon Americano? Go ahead and start ordering the Peppermint Latte. Trust me! You're just being proactive! You've gotta get your gut ready for the absurd amount of sugar and carbs you're going to be enjoying in the next month. Diet starts today—I believe in you!

GET WRAPPING. It's time to start wrapping all of the amazing gifts you're handing out this year. Did your stash of paper get damaged or used up last year? Well, here's a new idea: Buy some brown craft paper, wrap your gifts in it, and go crazy with those stamps you bought to make your one-of-a-kind holiday cards. Wrap as you buy and you'll be sitting pretty on Christmas morning (and your gifts will be, too!).

One Week Out

ATTEND THE OFFICE CHRISTMAS PARTY. Ah, work holiday parties. They're either too boozy or not boozy enough; too early in the day or so late that you feel like you're working longer than you would if there wasn't a party (and don't even get me started on the dreaded weekend work party); boring or just plain awkward. There's no getting around them, though, so here's a short, helpful list of office party dos and don'ts.

* *Do:* Bring a small gift for your direct supervisor. How about a monogrammed mug and a fancy tin of tea?

* *Don't:* Drink any sort of "Holiday Punch" or cocktail

made with more than one type of alcohol. You'll thank me later.

* *Do:* Have another engagement that you "can't miss" so you have an early exit plan, lest the office holiday happy hour turn into karaoke and shots with these people who have to see the next morning.

* *Don't:* Under any circumstances, partake in said karaoke. Just, don't.

* **Do:** Try to have fun! Be thankful for your coworkers (and the fact that holiday "break" is just around the corner).

 ## Three Days Before

MAKE COOKIES! Set aside a day to bake up a storm. Pick three of your favorite recipes, whip up a triple batch of each, and divvy them out onto paper plates. Wrap in cellophane or a piece of cloth, tie with a ribbon, and *voila*: hostess gifts on hand for all those parties you're surely going to, you festive thing.

Christmas Eve Eve

DO NOTHING. That is your only task on this day before the BIG day. Just… sit around. Go see a movie, watch the snow fall, eat some of those cookies you worked so hard on. Tempted to go to the mall for a last-minute gift? Not this year. Today, you do *nothing*.

Christmas Eve

GO CAROLING. Nothing will get you in the spirit faster than singing Christmas songs with your friends and family. Best of all, you're singing in a group and to strangers, no one cares if you can sing or not, they're just happy you're out there spreading Christmas cheer. Make sure you bring plenty of print-outs of lyrics so folks can join you along the way—and they will! Who can resist a traveling group of carolers? Pack a thermos of hot chocolate and you'll surely win the award for MVC (that's most valuable caroler).

MAKE BREAKFAST AHEAD. Take the time on Christmas Eve to make breakfast so you don't have to do anything Christmas morning except hit the preheat button on your oven. Strata is a super simple: cut up a loaf of bread and put in a casserole dish, pour a creamy egg-milk mixture over the bread, add in some toppings (spinach, bacon, cheese, red and green peppers), cover the dish and set it in the fridge overnight. Throw it in the oven the next morning before the gift giving begins and you'll have a hot, delicious breakfast ready by the time you're done opening presents. You're such a smart elf.

Wee Hours of the Morning

WRAP THE REST OF YOUR GIFTS.
For the most part, you've followed this guide and you're feeling prepped, relaxed, and ready to enjoy Christmas with your friends and family, right? But we're all human, and we all find ourselves in this position every once in a while. The back of your closet has been stacked with bags and boxes

and you kept saying you'd get to it, but you got pulled away—by the cookie baking! And the Christmas tree decorating! And the caroling! It's fine. Have a cup of coffee, throw on *White Christmas* or *It's a Wonderful Life*, and do what you need to do. Enjoy this quiet night before Christmas because let's face it: it's basically a tradition at this point.

YOU MADE IT! Breakfast is warming up; your adorable hand-made wrapping paper is in ripped, crumpled heaps around the living room; the teeny-tiny tinsel tree is glowing from its perch above a roaring fire; and there are batteries to be found and socks to be tried on. Good work. Only thing left to do now is sit back and enjoy. Merry, merry Christmas!

Day After Christmas

START THINKING ABOUT NEXT YEAR'S CHRISTMAS:
It's only 364 days away!

This book has been bound
using handcraft methods and
Smyth-sewn to ensure durability.

The box and interior were
designed by Ashley Todd.

The text was written
by Mollie Thomas.